AMERICAN

HERITAGE®

dic·tion·ar·y

Define·a·Thon™

FOR THE

HIGH
SCHOOL

GRADUATE

Houghton Mifflin

BOSTON · NEW YORK

Visit our websites: www.ahdictionary.com *or* www.houghtonmifflinbooks.com

Library of Congress Cataloging-in-Publication Data

The American Heritage Dictionary define-a-thon for the high school graduate.
  p. cm.
 ISBN-13: 978-0-618-90875-2
 ISBN-10: 0-618-90875-7
 1. Vocabulary--Problems, exercises, etc. I. Title: Define-a-thon for the high school graduate.
 PE1449.A463 2007
 428.1--dc22

2007014626

Text design by Anne Chalmers
Typefaces: Memphis, Minion, Frutiger

Manufactured in the United States of America

EB 10 9 8 7 6 5 4 3 2 1

Contents

Define-α-Thon
Word Challenge
1

Define-α-Thon
Word Challenge
R E V E A L E D
15

Define-α-Thon
Answer Key
87

EDITORIAL STAFF
of the *American Heritage® Dictionaries*

Margery S. Berube, *Vice President, Publisher of Dictionaries*

Joseph P. Pickett, *Vice President, Executive Editor*

Steven R. Kleinedler, *Supervising Editor*

Susan I. Spitz, *Senior Editor*

Catherine Pratt, *Editor*

Patrick Taylor, *Editor*

Nicholas A. Durlacher, *Associate Editor*

Louise E. Robbins, *Associate Editor*

Peter Chipman, *Assistant Editor*

Preface

The editors of the American Heritage dictionaries are pleased to present *The American Heritage Dictionary Define-a-Thon for the High School Graduate*, a new kind of brain teaser that will challenge students to reach for a more sophisticated vocabulary while at the same time bolstering their dictionary skills to foster more independent learning.

The challenge is both simple and subtle. Each question consists of a definition and four candidate words, only one of which is correct. The editors have carefully selected both the definitions and the words listed beneath them with the high school graduate in mind, since all the words can be found in the reading and curriculum of the junior and senior years of high school. The words are often similar in sound or form to one another, so you must think not only about the correct choice to each question but also about the meaning of the other choices as well.

Define-a-Thon for the High School Graduate is more than a quiz book, however. It's also a platform for learning about words. The Word Challenge Revealed section that follows the Word Challenge itself provides fascinating background information about each correct word, while also explaining what the other words in the group mean. Each correct word is shown in an example sentence and accompanied by an etymology explaining the historical development of the word, which usually comes from another language such as Latin, Greek, or German. The etymology provides deeper insight into the meaning of the word and can be a helpful aid to remembering what the word means in English today.

Some words have remarkable stories that can't be conveyed easily in an etymology. These stories are told in separate paragraphs and make for fascinating reading. For other words, still more help appears in the form of quotations from authors who are typically read during the high school years.

The editors of the American Heritage dictionaries encourage you to incorporate the words presented in this book into your own vocabulary. The more powerful your vocabulary becomes, the easier it will be for you to express what you are thinking clearly and effectively—wherever you may be.

So take up the Define-a-Thon challenge and improve your knowledge of English! No matter how you play—alone, with friends, or with family—you are sure to end up a winner!

— Joe Pickett
Executive Editor
— Steve Kleinedler
Supervising Editor

Guide to the
Define-a-Thon

The first part of the book, the Define-a-Thon Word Challenge, consists of a series of definitions. Each definition is followed by four possible answers. Only one of these answers is correct. It is your job to determine the correct answer.

The second part, the Define-a-Thon Word Challenge Revealed, is much more than an answer key. It provides you with a wealth of information about the words used in the Define-a-Thon. For each word that is the correct answer, we provide a sentence to show how this word is used in context. Additionally, we show the etymology of the word, so you can learn how this word entered the English language. Occasionally the etymology will contain a word that is not actually preserved in written documents but that scholars are confident did exist; such a form will be marked by an asterisk (*). We also provide the definition for each word that is an incorrect answer, so you can learn the meanings of all the words and see how they differ.

Some entries include notes that present interesting information regarding the history of the word, including the process by which it entered English from other languages. Other entries include quotations from works of literature to show how well-established writers have used the word in both classic and contemporary texts.

Following the Define-a-Thon Word Challenge Revealed is a simple answer key that lists the correct answers at a glance.

Reading and understanding this material is a fun and easy way to incorporate useful new words into your active vocabulary.

Define-a-Thon
Word Challenge

1. A long, roofed porch that runs along one or more sides of a building.

alcove   foyer

turret   veranda

2. Very careful; precise.

meticulous   nebulous

ridiculous   scrupulous

3. Not capable of making a mistake.

crestfallen   fallacious

fallow   infallible

4. To make a loud, strong verbal attack or de-nunciation.

allocate   fulminate

masticate   prognosticate

5. A legendary serpent or dragon that could kill with its breath and glance.

basilisk   moa

ptarmigan   roc

6. Stopping and starting at intervals; not continuous.

> interactive   interminable
>
> intermittent   interrogative

7. To move in waves or with a smooth, wavy motion.

> emanate   insinuate
>
> permeate   undulate

8. Relating to or occurring in a 24-hour period; daily.

> didactic   dilatory
>
> diurnal   divergent

9. A liquid medicine rubbed on the skin to soothe pain or relieve stiffness, as from bruises or sore muscles.

> astringent   liniment
>
> raiment   solvent

10. A ring or loop hanging by a strap from a horse's saddle to support a rider's foot.

> chaparral   garrison
>
> stirrup   vaquero

11. A hurricane occurring in the western Pacific or Indian Oceans.

tornado   tsunami

turbulence   typhoon

12. The ratio of the length of the side adjacent to an acute angle of a right triangle to the length of the hypotenuse.

area   cosine

sine   tangent

13. Any of a group of hormones present in the brain that affect various bodily responses, such as pain or emotion.

endorphin   hemoglobin

neuron   vitamin

14. A humorous nickname.

aqueduct   marquee

parquet   sobriquet

15. A word, phrase, verse, or sentence that reads the same backward or forward.

acrostic   analogy

innuendo   palindrome

---

16. To make something so confusing or murky that it is hard to understand or see.

obfuscate   obligate

obtrude   obviate

17. Of, relating to, or based on the number 12.

binary   duodecimal

hexadecimal   octal

18. A high ridge of land or rock jutting out into a body of water.

peninsula   plateau

promontory   tundra

19. To make useless or ineffectual.

edify   mollify

stultify   vilify

20. Violation of allegiance toward one's country or sovereign, especially the betrayal of one's country by waging war against it or by consciously and purposely acting to aid its enemies.

assault   perjury

slander   treason

21. Free from living microorganisms causing infection.

anemic   aseptic

in vitro   in vivo

22. The process of giving off small bubbles of gas.

aeration   effervescence

evanescence   sublimation

23. To criticize someone for misbehavior or a personal fault.

rebut   repent

reprove   requite

24. A song of a Venetian gondolier with a rhythm that suggests rowing.

barcarole   imbroglio

mazurka   palazzo

25. A jellylike substance that forms the living matter in all plant and animal cells.

cellulose   DNA

mitochondria   protoplasm

26. A supplement or appendix, especially to a will.

     codicil   prospectus

     subscript   synopsis

27. A written declaration made under oath before a notary public or other authorized officer.

     affidavit   indictment

     inquisition   subpoena

28. A deciduous, dioecious tree native to China and having fan-shaped leaves and fleshy, yellowish seeds with a disagreeable odor.

     Asiago   eryngo

     ginkgo   mofongo

29. A set of bells hung in a tower, usually played from a keyboard.

     caisson   carillon

     chorion   cotillion

30. Critical explanation or analysis, especially of a text.

     denotation   exegesis

     exemplar   pellucidity

31. In law, to set aside or annul.

> quash   remand
>
> suborn   suppress

32. A covered litter carried on poles on the shoulders of four or more bearers, formerly used in eastern Asia.

> harlequin   lambrequin
>
> palanquin   spillikin

33. Smelling of mildew or decay; moldy.

> decadent   fusty
>
> numinous   reticulate

34. A short piece of music played between sections of a long musical work.

> interim   intermezzo
>
> mezzaluna   mezzanine

35. The tendency of a body at rest to remain at rest, or of a body in motion to continue moving in a straight line at a constant speed unless a force is applied to it.

> gravity   inertia
>
> momentum   velocity

36. To undergo a rapid twitching of muscle fibers, especially of the heart.

coruscate   enervate

extirpate   fibrillate

37. The capacity to live, grow, or develop.

vigilance   visibility

vitality   vituperation

38. Dissatisfied with existing conditions.

maladjusted   maladroit

malcontent   malevolent

39. The number 10 raised to the 100th power, written as 10^{100} or as 1 followed by 100 zeros.

exponent   googol

infinity   sextillion

40. A computer security system designed to prevent unauthorized people from gaining access to a computer network.

cordon   firewall

moat   motherboard

41. An association of independent business firms, often from different countries, organized to control prices, production, and sales by its members.

cartel   guild

mélange   monopoly

42. The long bone of the leg between the knee and pelvis in humans; the thighbone.

coccyx   femur

ulna   viola

43. A person who attacks and opposes popular or traditional ideas, beliefs, or practices.

iconoclast   ideologue

intercessor   introvert

44. Being quiet, still, or at rest; inactive.

amenable   quiescent

secular   sinister

45. A medieval instrument formerly used to determine the altitude of the sun and other celestial bodies.

astrolabe   cosmos

guillotine   heliotrope

46. The branch of zoology that deals with the study of fishes.

    herpetology   ichthyology

    ornithology   speleology

47. An idea or symbol that recurs in a literary or artistic work.

    metaphor   motif

    paradigm   trope

48. Appearance, especially the expression of the face.

    appurtenance   consonance

    countenance   repugnance

49. Measured rhythmic flow, as of poetry or oratory.

    cadence   manifesto

    syntax   timbre

50. A part of the brain, located at the rear of the skull, that regulates balance and coordinates muscle activity.

    cambium   cerebellum

    cerebrum   cesium

51. Implied from actions; not spoken or written.

    ambiguous   cryptic

        pallid   tacit

52. A plant stem that grows under or along the ground and that sends out shoots and roots.

    chloroplast   phloem

      rhizome   stamen

53. Arousing fear, dread, or alarm.

    dubious   formidable

    incendiary   noisome

54. A line whose distance to a given curve gets closer and closer to zero.

    asymptote   axis

      focus   theorem

55. A branching part of a nerve cell that receives and transmits cell impulses.

    axon   boron

    dendrite   ganglion

56. A stopping of some activity for the time being; a temporary ban or pause.

crematorium   moratorium

natatorium   sanatorium

57. A shoulder ornament, especially a fringed strap worn on military uniforms.

epaulet   epitaph

epoch   epsilon

58. Cheerfully confident; optimistic.

choleric   melancholy

phlegmatic   sanguine

Define-a-Thon
Word Challenge
R E V E A L E D

The Radley Place jutted into a sharp curve beyond our house. Walking south, one faced its porch; the sidewalk turned and ran beside the lot. The house was low, was once white with a deep front porch and green shutters, but had long ago darkened to the color of the slate-gray yard around it. Rain-rotted shingles drooped over the eaves of the **veranda**; oak trees kept the sun away. The remains of a picket drunkenly guarded the front yard—a "swept" yard that was never swept—where johnson grass and rabbit-tobacco grew in abundance.

—Harper Lee
To Kill a Mockingbird

1.

veranda

A long, roofed porch that runs along one or more sides of a building.

In the summer, we would sit on the veranda late into the evening, drinking lemonade and telling stories.

[From Hindi *varaṇḍā*, probably from Portuguese *varanda*, balcony, porch.]

WHAT THE OTHER WORDS MEAN

alcove: A small room opening on a larger one without being separated from it by a wall or door.

foyer: An entrance hall, as of a private house or apartment.

turret: A small tower or tower-shaped projection on a building.

meticulous

Very careful; precise.

The editor paid meticulous attention to the manuscript to make sure every word was properly spelled.

[From Latin *metīculōsus*, timid, from *metus*, fear.]

WHAT THE OTHER WORDS MEAN

nebulous: Lacking a definite shape or form; unclear or vague.

ridiculous: Very silly.

scrupulous: Careful and honest.

infallible

Not capable of making a mistake.

We thought the computer program was infallible, so we were surprised when it produced the wrong answer.

[From Middle English, from Medieval Latin *īnfallibilis* : Latin *in-*, not + Medieval Latin *fallibilis*, fallible, liable to be deceived, from Latin *fallere*, to deceive.]

WHAT THE OTHER WORDS MEAN

crestfallen: Dejected; depressed.

fallacious: Based on a false notion or mistaken belief.

fallow: Plowed and tilled but left unseeded during a growing season.

4.

fulminate

To make a loud, strong verbal attack or denunciation.

The speaker fulminated against the waste of natural resources.

[From Middle English *fulminaten*, from Latin *fulmināre*, *fulmināt-*, to strike with lightning, from *fulmen*, *fulmin-*, lightning that strikes, thunderbolt.]

WHAT THE OTHER WORDS MEAN

allocate: To set aside for a particular purpose; allot.

masticate: To chew food.

prognosticate: To predict on the basis of present signs or symptoms.

5.

basilisk

A legendary serpent or dragon that could kill with its breath and glance.

According to legend, one can kill a basilisk by holding a mirror up to its face so that it is slain by the reflection of its own glance.

[From Middle English, from Old French *basilisc*, from Latin *basiliscus*, from Greek *basiliskos*, kinglet, basilisk (said to have a crownlike mark on its head), from *basileus*, king.]

WHAT THE OTHER WORDS MEAN

moa: Any of various flightless ostrichlike birds of the family Dinornithidae, native to New Zealand and extinct for over a century.

ptarmigan: Any of various grouses inhabiting arctic, subarctic, and alpine regions of the Northern Hemisphere and having feathered legs and feet and plumage that is brown or gray in summer and white in winter.

roc: A mythical bird of prey having enormous size and strength.

intermittent

Stopping and starting at intervals; not continuous.

The foghorn sounded intermittent blasts at intervals of 15 seconds.

[From Latin *intermittēns, intermittent-*, present participle of Latin *intermittere*, to leave off, pause : *inter-*, between, in the midst of + *mittere*, to let go.]

WHAT THE OTHER WORDS MEAN

interactive: Relating to a computer program that responds to user activity.

interminable: Having or seeming to have no end; endless.

interrogative: Asking a question or having the nature of a question.

It was the best of nationally advertised and quantitatively produced alarm-clocks, with all modern attachments, including cathedral chime, **intermittent** alarm, and a phosphorescent dial. Babbitt was proud of being awakened by such a rich device. Socially it was almost as creditable as buying expensive cord tires.

—Sinclair Lewis
Babbitt

undulate

To move in waves or with a smooth, wavy motion.

The fronds of the palm tree undulated in the light breeze.

[From Late Latin *undula*, small wave, diminutive of Latin *unda*, wave.]

WHAT THE OTHER WORDS MEAN

emanate: To come forth, as from a source.

insinuate: To introduce or suggest in a sly or indirect way.

permeate: To spread or flow throughout.

diurnal

Relating to or occurring in a 24-hour period; daily.

Many marine organisms exhibit diurnal migration, moving deeper in the water during the day and closer to the surface during the night.

[From Middle English *diurnal*, from Late Latin *diurnālis*, from Latin *diurnus*, relating to the day, daily, from *diēs*, day.]

WHAT THE OTHER WORDS MEAN

didactic: Intended to instruct.

dilatory: Tending to postpone or delay.

divergent: Drawing apart from a common point; diverging.

9.

liniment

A liquid medicine rubbed on the skin to soothe pain or relieve stiffness, as from bruises or sore muscles.

After the child fell, his mother rubbed some soothing liniment on his bruised shin.

[From Middle English, from Late Latin *linīmentum*, from Latin *linere, linīre*, to rub over, anoint.]

WHAT THE OTHER WORDS MEAN

astringent: A substance, such as alum, that draws together or contracts body tissues and thus checks the flow of blood or other secretions.

raiment: Clothing; garments.

solvent: A liquid that is capable of dissolving another substance.

stirrup

A ring or loop hanging by a strap from a horse's saddle to support a rider's foot.

The cowboy mounted the horse by putting his right foot in the stirrup and swinging his left leg over the horse's back.

[From Middle English *stirope*, from Old English *stīgrāp* : *stīgan*, to mount + *rāp*, rope.]

WHAT THE OTHER WORDS MEAN

chaparral: A group of low, tangled bushes growing close together over a wide area of land, especially in the southwest United States and Mexico.

garrison: A military base.

vaquero: A cowboy.

11.

typhoon

A hurricane occurring in the western Pacific or Indian Oceans.

Strong winds and heavy rains lashed Taiwan as the typhoon approached.

[Ultimately from Greek *tuphōn*, whirlwind, Arabic *ṭūfōn*, deluge (from Greek *tuphōn*), and Cantonese *taaîfung* (equivalent to Mandarin *tái*, great + Mandarin *fēng*, wind).]

WHAT THE OTHER WORDS MEAN

tornado: A violent, rotating column of air ranging in width from a few yards to more than a mile.

tsunami: A very large ocean wave that is caused by an underwater earthquake or volcanic eruption and often causes extreme destruction when it strikes land.

turbulence: An eddying motion of the atmosphere that interrupts the flow of wind.

With elements of Greek, Arabic, Chinese, and Indian languages in its background, **typhoon** shows the twisted, stormy paths that words can take as they pass from language to language. Greek *tuphōn* was both a common noun meaning "whirlwind, typhoon," and the name of a mythological monster, Typhon. *Tuphōn* was borrowed into Arabic as *ṭūfān*, "inundation, deluge," and when Arabic-speaking Muslims settled in India beginning in the 11th century, *ṭūfān* was borrowed into various languages of India. Hindi *tūfān*, for example, means "a storm of wind and rain." By 1588, the Indian word had passed into English as *touffon*. Around the same time, English voyagers were sailing beyond India to China, where they encountered the Cantonese word for the powerful tropical cyclones that occur in the waters around China, *taaîfung*, as well as related words in other Chinese dialects. The Chinese word, recorded in such spellings as *ty-foong*, entered English by 1699. Eventually, the two similar words meaning "strong storm"—one from Arabic and the other from Chinese—coalesced to give the English word *typhoon*.

cosine

The ratio of the length of the side adjacent to an acute angle of a right triangle to the length of the hypotenuse.

As an angle increases from 0 degrees to 90 degrees, its cosine decreases from 1 to 0.

[From *co-*, together, jointly + *sine*, from Medieval Latin *sinus*, sine (used in Medieval Latin to translate the Arabic mathematical term *jayb*, sine, literally meaning hollow, pocket), from Latin *sinus*, curve, fold in a toga used as a pocket.]

WHAT THE OTHER WORDS MEAN

area:
: The extent of a surface or plane figure as measured in square units.

sine:
: The ratio of the length of the side opposite an acute angle of a right triangle to the length of the hypotenuse.

tangent:
: The ratio of the length of the side opposite an acute angle of a right triangle to the length of the side adjacent to that angle.

endorphin

Any of a group of hormones present in the brain that affect various bodily responses, such as pain or emotion.

The researchers claimed that eating chocolate makes people feel good because it triggers the release of endorphins.

[From *endo(genous)* + *(mo)rphin(e)*.]

WHAT THE OTHER WORDS MEAN

hemoglobin: The substance, made up of protein and iron, that gives the red blood cells of vertebrates their characteristic color. Hemoglobin carries oxygen from the lungs to body tissues and carries carbon dioxide from the tissues to the lungs.

neuron: A nerve cell.

vitamin: Any of various complex organic compounds that are needed in small amounts for normal growth and activity of the body and are found naturally in foods obtained from plants and animals.

14.

sobriquet

A humorous nickname.

The baseball player Joe DiMaggio earned the sobriquet "Joltin' Joe" after a record hitting streak.

[From French *sobriquet*, from earlier *sobriquet*, joking, mockery, from Old French *soubriquet*, a chuck under the chin.]

WHAT THE OTHER WORDS MEAN

aqueduct: A large pipe or channel that carries water from a distant source.

marquee: A structure that projects over the entrance to a building, such as a theater or hotel, and often bears a signboard.

parquet: A floor made of wood, often of contrasting colors, worked into a pattern or mosaic.

15.

palindrome

A word, phrase, verse, or sentence that reads the same backward or forward.

"Madam, I'm Adam" is a well-known example of a palindrome.

[From Greek *palindromos*, running back again, recurring : *palin*, again + *dromos*, a running.]

WHAT THE OTHER WORDS MEAN

acrostic: A poem or series of lines in which certain letters, usually the first in each line, spell out a name, phrase, or message.

analogy: An explanation of something by comparing it with something similar.

innuendo: An indirect hint or suggestion, usually intended to hurt the good name or standing of someone; an insinuation.

16.
obfuscate

To make something so confusing or murky that it is hard to understand or see.

The report was so complicated that it obfuscated the findings rather than making them clear.

[From Latin *obfuscāre, obfuscāt-*, to darken : *ob-*, over + *fuscāre*, to darken (from *fuscus*, dark).]

WHAT THE OTHER WORDS MEAN

obligate: To bind, compel, or constrain by a social, legal, or moral tie.

obtrude: To force ideas or opinions upon another without invitation.

obviate: To anticipate and prevent; make unnecessary.

17.

duodecimal

Of, relating to, or based on the number 12.

The duodecimal system uses the digits 0, 1, 2, 3, 4, 5, 6, 7, 8, 9, A, and B.

[From Latin *duodecimus*, twelfth, from *duodecim*, twelve : *duo*, two + *decem*, ten.]

WHAT THE OTHER WORDS MEAN

binary: Of, relating to, or based on the number 2.

hexadecimal: Of, relating to, or based on the number 16.

octal: Of, relating to, or based on the number 8.

I have of late—but wherefore I know not—
lost all my mirth, forgone all custom of exercises; and indeed it goes so heavily with
my disposition, that this goodly frame, the
earth, seems to me a sterile **promontory**;
this most excellent canopy, the air, look
you, this brave o'erhanging firmament, this
majestical roof fretted with golden fire,
why, it appeareth nothing to me but a foul
and pestilent congregation of vapors.
What a piece of work is a man, how noble
in reason, how infinite in faculties, in form
and moving, how express and admirable
in action, how like an angel in apprehen-
sion, how like a god! the beauty of the
world; the paragon of animals; and yet
to me what is this quintessence of dust?
Man delights not me—nor woman neither,
though by your smiling you seem to say so.

—William Shakespeare
Hamlet (Act 2, Scene 2)

18.

promontory

A high ridge of land or rock jutting out
into a body of water.

*She stood on the promontory and
enjoyed the view out over the bay.*

[From Latin *prōmontorium*, promontory, alteration
(influenced by *mōns, mont-*, mountain) of *prōmun-
turium*, probably from *prōminēre*, to jut out.]

WHAT THE OTHER WORDS MEAN

peninsula: A piece of land that projects
into a body of water and is
connected with a larger land
mass.

plateau: An elevated, comparatively
level expanse of land.

tundra: A cold, treeless area of arctic
regions, having permanently
frozen subsoil and only low-
growing mosses, lichens, and
stunted shrubs as plant life.

stultify

To make useless or ineffectual.

*The rigid standardized tests stulti-
fied the students' creativity.*

[From Late Latin *stultificāre*, to make foolish : Latin
stultus, foolish + Latin *-ficāre*, to cause to become,
make (from *facere*, to do).]

WHAT THE OTHER WORDS MEAN

edify: To instruct so as to encourage
intellectual, moral, or spiritual
improvement.

mollify: To lessen the anger of; placate.

vilify: To make vicious and defama-
tory statements about.

20.

treason

Violation of allegiance toward one's country or sovereign, especially the betrayal of one's country by waging war against it or by consciously and purposely acting to aid its enemies.

Anthony Babington was convicted of treason and executed in 1586 for plotting to assassinate Elizabeth I and to place Mary Queen of Scots on the throne.

[From Middle English, from Anglo-Norman *treson,* from Latin *trāditiō, trāditiōn-,* a handing over, from *trāditus,* past participle of *trādere,* to hand over, deliver, entrust : *trāns-, trā-,* across + *dare,* to give.]

WHAT THE OTHER WORDS MEAN

assault: An unlawful attempt or threat to injure another physically.

perjury: The deliberate giving of false, misleading, or incomplete testimony while under oath.

slander: The act or crime of reporting or uttering a false statement maliciously to damage someone's reputation.

21.
aseptic

Free from living microorganisms causing infection.

After aseptic techniques were adopted in operating rooms, postoperative mortality rates decreased.

[From *a-*, not + *septic* (from Latin *sēpticus,* putrefying, from Greek *sēptikos,* from *sēptos,* rotten, from *sēpein,* to make rotten).]

WHAT THE OTHER WORDS MEAN

anemic: Having a medical condition in which the blood cannot carry enough oxygen to the body tissues.

in vitro: In an artificial environment outside a living organism.

in vivo: Within a living organism.

effervescence

The process of giving off small bubbles of gas.

The soda sparkled in the glass because of the effervescence.

[From Latin *effervēscere* : *ex-,* up, out + *fervēscere,* to start boiling, from *fervēre,* to boil.]

WHAT THE OTHER WORDS MEAN

aeration: The process of supplying something with oxygen.

evanescence: The tendency to vanish or last only a short time.

sublimation: The process of causing a solid or gas to change state without becoming liquid.

reprove

To criticize someone for misbehavior or a personal fault.

With a quick look, the teacher reproved the child for whispering in class.

[From Middle English *reproven*, from Old French *reprover*, from Late Latin *reprobāre*, to disapprove : Latin *re-*, opposite of + *probāre*, to approve (from *probus*, good).]

WHAT THE OTHER WORDS MEAN

rebut: To prove something false, especially by presenting opposing evidence or arguments.

repent: To feel remorse or regret for what one has done or failed to do.

requite: To make repayment or return for; reciprocate.

At last there was something to do in those long, empty summer evenings, when the married people sat like images on their front porches, and the boys and girls tramped and tramped the board sidewalks. . . . Now there was a place where the girls could wear their new dresses, and where one could laugh aloud without being **reproved** by the ensuing silence. That silence seemed to ooze out of the ground, to hang under the foliage of the black maple trees with the bats and shadows.

—Willa Cather
My Ántonia

barcarole

A song of a Venetian gondolier with a rhythm that suggests rowing.

The tourists were enthralled when their gondolier began to sing a lilting barcarole.

[From French, from Italian *barcaruola,* from *barcaruolo,* gondolier, from *barca,* boat, from Latin *barca.*]

WHAT THE OTHER WORDS MEAN

imbroglio: A confused or difficult situation; a predicament.

mazurka: A Polish dance that resembles the polka.

palazzo: A large, splendid residence or public building, such as a palace or museum.

25.

protoplasm

A jellylike substance that forms the living matter in all plant and animal cells.

The scientist described the human brain as three pounds of protoplasm.

[From German *Protoplasma*, protoplasm, from Greek *prōtos*, first, primitive + *plasma*, molded thing, figure (from *plassein*, to mold).]

WHAT THE OTHER WORDS MEAN

cellulose: A carbohydrate that is insoluble in water, forms the main component of plant tissues, and is used in making a variety of products, such as paper, cellophane, textiles, and explosives.

DNA: An acid found in all living cells having a structure resembling a ladder that is twisted into a spiral and forming the main part of chromosomes.

mitochrondria: Microscopic structures found in the cytoplasm of almost all living cells, containing enzymes that act in converting food to usable energy.

---

codicil

A supplement or appendix, especially to a will.

She added a codicil to her will that set aside funds for the care of her dogs.

[From Middle English, from Old French *codicille*, from Latin *cōdicillus*, diminutive of *cōdex, cōdic-*, wooden tablet, book, variant of *caudex*, tree trunk.]

WHAT THE OTHER WORDS MEAN

prospectus: A printed description of a business or other venture.

subscript: A symbol or character written directly beneath or next to and slightly below another symbol or character, as in a mathematical expression or chemical formula.

synopsis: A brief summary or outline of a subject or written work.

affidavit

A written declaration made under oath before a notary public or other authorized officer.

A replacement check will not be issued until you sign an affidavit stating that you never received the original check.

[From Medieval Latin *affīdāvit*, he has stated on oath, third person singular perfect tense of *affīdāre*, to state on oath : Latin *ad-*, *af-*, to, towards + Vulgar Latin **fīdāre*, to trust (from *fīdus*, trustworthy).]

WHAT THE OTHER WORDS MEAN

indictment: A written statement charging a party with the commission of a crime or other offense, drawn up by a prosecuting attorney and found and presented by a grand jury.

inquisition: An investigation, especially one that violates the privacy or rights of individuals.

subpoena: A writ requiring a person to appear in court and give testimony.

28.

ginkgo

A deciduous, dioecious tree native to China and having fan-shaped leaves and fleshy, yellowish seeds with a disagreeable odor.

Ginkgos can tolerate urban environments and are often grown as ornamental trees that line streets.

[Probably a misreading of Japanese *ginkyō*, which is itself an archaic or artificial literary reading of the Chinese characters used to write the word for the ginkgo in Japanese : *gin*, silver (from Middle Chinese ŋin) + *kyō*, apricot (from Middle Chinese γəïjŋ́, apricot).]

WHAT THE OTHER WORDS MEAN

Asiago: A yellow Italian cheese suitable for grating when aged.

eryngo: Any of several related plants having spiny leaves and dense clusters of small, bluish flowers.

mofongo: A Puerto Rican dish made of mashed plantains, garlic, and pork cracklings.

The odd spelling of **ginkgo** may result from a botanist's error. The Japanese word for the edible seeds of the ginkgo is written with two Chinese characters that can be read as *ginkyō*, meaning "silver apricot." (The characters probably refer to the yellowish-green fruitlike structures produced by the tree, inside of which the nuts are surrounded by a white shell like a pistachio's.) In Modern Japanese, however, *ginkyō* is not the usual word for the ginkgo—the nuts are called *ginnan*, while the tree is called *itchō*.

The first European to learn of the ginkgo tree was Engelbert Kaempfer (1651–1716), a German physician who visited Japan in 1691. After his death, Kaempfer's extensive notes on Japan were edited and published as a book that became an essential reference work in the West. However, it is said that Kaempfer had bad handwriting, and at some point his transliteration of Japanese *ginkyō* was misread as *ginkgo*. The great Swedish botanist Carl von Linné perpetuated the error when he gave the scientific name *Ginkgo biloba* to the tree.

29.
carillon

A set of bells hung in a tower, usually played from a keyboard.

When the carillon in the cathedral was played, the sound rang out across the countryside.

[From French *carillon*, from Old French *quarellon*, alteration of *quarregnon*, set of four bells, from Late Latin *quaterniō*, *quaterniōn-*, set of four, from Latin *quater*, four times, akin to *quattuor*, four.]

WHAT THE OTHER WORDS MEAN

caisson: A watertight structure in which underwater construction work is done, as in the building of tunnels, bridges, or dams.

chorion: The outer membrane that encloses the embryo of a reptile, bird, or mammal.

cotillion: A formal ball, especially one at which young women are presented to society.

exegesis

Critical explanation or analysis, especially of a text.

The rabbi was renowned for his brilliant exegesis of the Talmud.

[From Greek *exēgēsis*, from *exēgeisthai*, to interpret : *ex-*, out + *hēgeisthai*, to lead.]

WHAT THE OTHER WORDS MEAN

denotation: The most specific or direct meaning of a word, in contrast to its figurative or associated meanings.

exemplar: One that is worthy of imitation; a model.

pellucidity: Transparent clarity in style or meaning.

31.

quash

In law, to set aside or annul.

Citing new evidence, the appeals court quashed the governor's conviction on both charges.

[From Middle English *quassen*, to nullify, from Old French *casser*, *quasser*, from Medieval Latin *quassāre*, alteration (influenced by *quassāre*, to shatter) of *cassāre*, from Latin *cassus*, empty, void.]

WHAT THE OTHER WORDS MEAN

remand: To send back a legal case to a lower court for further proceedings.

suborn: To cause someone to commit an unlawful or evil act.

suppress: To restrict or forbid the activities of.

32.

palanquin

A covered litter carried on poles on the shoulders of four or more bearers, formerly used in eastern Asia.

The queen was carried to the palace in a magnificent gold palanquin.

[From Portuguese *palanquim*, ultimately from a source in a language of India akin to Hindi *pālkī*, from Prakrit *pallaṅka*, from Sanskrit *paryaṅkaḥ*, *palyaṅkaḥ*, couch, palanquin.]

WHAT THE OTHER WORDS MEAN

harlequin: A conventional buffoon of the commedia dell'arte, traditionally presented in a mask and a multicolored costume.

lambrequin: A short ornamental drapery for the top of a window or door or the edge of a shelf.

spillikin: A long, thin stick used in a game in which players attempt to remove each stick from a pile one at a time without disturbing the others.

It was a queer, sultry summer, the summer they electrocuted the Rosenbergs, and I didn't know what I was doing in New York. I'm stupid about executions. The idea of being electrocuted makes me sick, and that's all there was to read about in the papers—goggle-eyed headlines staring up at me on every street corner and at the **fusty**, peanut-smelling mouth of every subway. It had nothing to do with me, but I couldn't help wondering what it would be like, being burned alive all along your nerves.

—Sylvia Plath
The Bell Jar

33.

fusty

Smelling of mildew or decay; moldy.

I couldn't identify the source of the fusty smell in the damp basement.

[From Middle English *fusty*, stale-smelling, smelling of the cask, from *fust*, wine cask, from Old French *fust*, piece of wood, wine cask, from Latin *fūstis*, stick, club.]

WHAT THE OTHER WORDS MEAN

decadent: In a condition of deterioration or decline.

numinous: Filled with or characterized by a sense of a supernatural presence.

reticulate: Resembling or forming a net or network.

intermezzo

A short piece of music played between sections of a long musical work.

Between acts of the opera, the orchestra played a brief, light-hearted intermezzo.

[From Italian *intermezzo*, from Latin *intermedius*, intermediate : Latin *inter-*, between + Latin *medius*, in the middle.]

WHAT THE OTHER WORDS MEAN

interim: An interval of time between two events, periods, or processes.

mezzaluna: A curved steel blade, often with a vertical handle at each end, used to chop food.

mezzanine: A partial story between two main stories of a building.

inertia

The tendency of a body at rest to remain at rest, or of a body in motion to continue moving in a straight line at a constant speed unless a force is applied to it.

Mass is a measure of a body's inertia.

[From Latin *inertia*, idleness, from *iners, inert-*, inert : *in-*, not + *ars, art-*, art, skill, employment.]

WHAT THE OTHER WORDS MEAN

gravity: The natural force of attraction exerted by a celestial body, such as the earth, upon objects at or near its surface, tending to draw them toward the center of the body.

momentum: A quantity used to measure the motion of a body, equal to the product of its mass and velocity. Any change in the speed or direction of a body changes its momentum.

velocity: The rate at which an object moves in a specified direction.

36.
fibrillate

To undergo a rapid twitching of muscle fibers, especially of the heart.

When the heart begins to fibrillate, it can sometimes be shocked back into a normal rhythm with a defibrillator.

[From New Latin *fibrilla*, fibril, muscle fiber (diminutive of Latin *fibra*, fiber) + English *-ate*, suffix forming verbs.]

WHAT THE OTHER WORDS MEAN

coruscate: To give forth flashes of light; sparkle.

enervate: To weaken or destroy the strength or vitality of.

extirpate: To destroy totally; exterminate.

vitality

The capacity to live, grow, or develop.

Because the plants were pruned badly, they lost their vitality.

[From Latin *vītālitās*, life force, vitality, from *vītālis*, relating to life, vital, from *vīta*, life.]

WHAT THE OTHER WORDS MEAN

vigilance: Alert watchfulness.

visibility: The fact that something can be seen or the degree to which something can be seen.

vituperation: Sustained, harshly abusive language.

malcontent

Dissatisfied with existing conditions.

We were malcontent when we saw how small and dark the hotel room was.

[From French *malcontent* : *mal-*, bad, badly (from Old French *mal*, from Latin *male*, badly, and *malus*, bad) + *content*, content, pleased (from Old French *content*, from Latin *contentus*, contented, past participle of *continēre*, to contain, keep still).]

WHAT THE OTHER WORDS MEAN

maladjusted: Poorly adjusted to the demands or stresses of daily living.

maladroit: Lacking skill; awkward or inept.

malevolent: Wishing harm to others; malicious.

In my senior year at Art and Design, I learned about the Futurists. I wanted to do something like they had done. The Futurists had been a **malcontent** group of artists at the beginning of the century who loved speed and thought war was good, the "hygiene of humanity." To them it was important to begin again. Culture was dead and it was time for something new. . . . I liked them because I could relate to their anger. I realized that by reinventing culture, they were reinventing themselves. I wanted to reinvent myself too.

—Ernesto Quiñonez
Bodega Dreams

googol

The number 10 raised to the 100th power, written as 10^{100} or as 1 followed by 100 zeros. Written out, a googol is 10,000, 000,000,000,000,000,000,000,000,000,000,000, 000,000,000,000,000,000,000,000,000,000,000, 000,000,000,000,000,000,000,000,000,000.

The number of atoms in the universe is still less than one googol.

[Coined around 1920 at the age of nine by Milton Sirotta, nephew of American mathematician Edward Kasner (1878–1955), who had asked his nephews to create a name for the number.]

WHAT THE OTHER WORDS MEAN

exponent: A number or symbol, placed to the right of and above the expression to which it applies, that indicates the number of times a mathematical expression is used as a factor. For example, the exponent 3 in 5^3 indicates $5 \times 5 \times 5$.

infinity: A space, extent of time, or quantity that has no limit.

sextillion: The number 10^{21} (that is, 1,000,000,000,000,000,000,000).

40.

firewall

A computer security system designed to prevent unauthorized people from gaining access to a computer network.

The secure firewall blocked the identity thieves from hacking into the company's database.

[From *firewall*, a wall to prevent the spread of fire.]

WHAT THE OTHER WORDS MEAN

cordon: A line of people, military posts, or ships stationed around an area to enclose or guard it.

moat: A deep, wide ditch, usually filled with water, typically surrounding a fortified medieval town, fortress, or castle as a protection against assault.

motherboard: The main printed circuit board in a personal computer. It contains the central processing unit, the main system memory, controllers for disk drives and other devices, serial and parallel ports, and sometimes expansion slots.

41.

cartel

An association of independent business firms, often from different countries, organized to control prices, production, and sales by its members.

When the cartel of coffee growers collapsed, the price of coffee beans dropped to an all-time low.

[From German *Kartell,* from French *cartel,* written challenge to a duel, written agreement between belligerent parties, from Italian *cartello,* notice, placard, diminutive of *carta,* paper, from Latin *charta, carta,* paper made from papyrus.]

WHAT THE OTHER WORDS MEAN

guild: An association of persons who share a trade or pursuit, formed to protect mutual interests and maintain standards.

mélange: A mixture.

monopoly: Complete control by one company of the means of producing or selling a product or service.

42.

femur

The long bone of the leg between the knee and pelvis in humans; the thighbone.

He fell while skiing and broke his femur.

[From Latin *femur*, thigh.]

WHAT THE OTHER WORDS MEAN

coccyx: A small, triangular bone found at the base of the spinal column in humans and in tailless apes.

ulna: The bone that in humans extends from the elbow to the wrist on the side of the arm opposite to the thumb.

viola: A stringed instrument of the violin family, slightly larger than a violin, tuned a fifth lower, and having a deeper tone.

iconoclast

A person who attacks and opposes popular or traditional ideas, beliefs, or practices.

The composers who abandoned conventional harmonies for the twelve-tone scale were regarded as iconoclasts.

[From French *iconoclaste*, from Medieval Greek *eikonoklastēs*, smasher of religious images : *eikōn*, *eikon-*, image, icon + Greek *-klastēs*, breaker (from Greek *klān*, *klas-*, to break).]

WHAT THE OTHER WORDS MEAN

ideologue: A person who advocates a set of doctrines or beliefs that form the basis of some system, especially a political or economic one.

intercessor: A person who entreats on behalf of another, especially by prayer or petition to God.

introvert: A person who is not very sociable or outgoing and who tends to be preoccupied with his or her own thoughts and feelings.

Although a modern **iconoclast** may serve a useful function by forcing people to reexamine their beliefs, the original iconoclasts destroyed countless works of art. *Eikonoklastēs*, the ancestor of our word, was first formed in Medieval Greek from the elements *eikōn*, "image, likeness," and –*klastēs*, "breaker," from *klān*, "to break." In the 8th and 9th centuries, some Christians of the Byzantine Empire objected strongly to the display and veneration of religious images, and they destroyed many sculptures and paintings in their zeal. During the Reformation, some Protestants also believed that images in churches were idolatrous, and works of art were again banned and destroyed. Around this time, Greek *eikonoklastēs* was borrowed into English as *iconoclast*, at first in reference to the Byzantine iconoclasts. Later, in the 19th century, *iconoclast* took on its modern secular sense, "a person who attacks and opposes popular or traditional ideas, beliefs, or practices."

quiescent

Being quiet, still, or at rest; inactive.

Bears are in a quiescent state when they hibernate during the winter.

[From Latin *quiēscēns, quiēscent-*, present participle of *quiēscere*, to rest, from *quiēs*, quiet.]

WHAT THE OTHER WORDS MEAN

amenable: Willing to respond to advice or authority; agreeable.

secular: Relating to the affairs of the world rather than spiritual.

sinister: Suggesting or threatening evil.

astrolabe

A medieval instrument formerly used to determine the altitude of the sun and other celestial bodies.

An astrolabe usually consists of a precisely engraved brass plate with an attached disk that can be rotated to the proper position.

[From Middle English *astrelabie*, from Old French *astrelabe*, from Medieval Latin *astrolabium*, from Greek *astrolabon*, planisphere : *astro-*, star (from *astēr*, star) + *lambanein*, *lab-*, to take, apprehend with the senses or mind.]

WHAT THE OTHER WORDS MEAN

cosmos: The universe regarded as an orderly, harmonious whole.

guillotine: A device consisting of a heavy blade held aloft between two upright guides and dropped to behead the person below.

heliotrope: Any of several garden plants having clusters of small, fragrant, purplish flowers.

---

ichthyology

The branch of zoology that deals with the study of fishes.

Ichthyology does not include the study of whales and porpoises, which are mammals.

[From Greek *ikhthūs*, fish + English *-logy*, study of (ultimately from Latin *-logia*, from Greek *-logiā*, from *logos*, word, speech, discourse).]

WHAT THE OTHER WORDS MEAN

herpetology: The branch of zoology that deals with the study of reptiles and amphibians.

ornithology: The branch of zoology that deals with the study of birds.

speleology: The scientific study of caves.

motif

An idea or symbol that recurs in a literary or artistic work.

The motif of the mysterious stranger is found throughout the author's works.

[From French *motif,* subject of a painting, motif, from Old French *motif,* motive, cause, from Late Latin *mōtīvus,* of motion, from Latin *mōtus,* past participle of *movēre,* to move.]

WHAT THE OTHER WORDS MEAN

metaphor: A figure of speech in which a word or phrase that is ordinarily associated with one thing is applied to something else, thus making a comparison between the two.

paradigm: An example of how something should be done or treated; a model.

trope: A figure of speech using words in nonliteral ways, such as a metaphor.

The apartment and furniture would have been nothing extraordinary as belonging to a homely, northern farmer, with a stubborn **countenance**, and stalwart limbs set out to advantage in knee-breeches and gaiters. Such an individual, seated in his armchair, his mug of ale frothing on the round table before him, is to be seen in any circuit of five or six miles among these hills, if you go at the right time, after dinner. But Mr. Heathcliff forms a singular contrast to his abode and style of living.

—Emily Brontë
Wuthering Heights

48.

countenance

Appearance, especially the expression of the face.

The building inspector's grim countenance meant bad news.

[From Middle English *contenaunce*, from Old French *contenance*, bearing, from *contenir*, to behave, from Latin *continēre*, to hold together : *com-*, *con-*, together + *tenēre*, to hold.]

WHAT THE OTHER WORDS MEAN

appurtenance: Something added to another, more important thing; an appendage; an accessory.

consonance: Agreement or harmony; accord.

repugnance: Extreme dislike or aversion.

cadence

Measured rhythmic flow, as of poetry or oratory.

Her poetry is characterized by quick, short cadences.

[From Middle English, from Old French *cadence*, from Old Italian *cadenza*, conclusion, rhythm, from Vulgar Latin *cadentia*, a falling, from Latin *cadēns, cadent-*, present participle of *cadere*, to fall.]

WHAT THE OTHER WORDS MEAN

manifesto: A public declaration of principles and aims, especially of a political nature.

syntax: The way in which words are put together to form phrases and sentences.

timbre: The combination of qualities of a sound that distinguishes it from other sounds of the same pitch and volume.

50.
cerebellum

A part of the brain, located at the rear of the skull, that regulates balance and co-ordinates muscle activity.

Children born with damage to the cerebellum have problems with movement.

[From Medieval Latin, from Latin *cerebellum*, little brain, brain (in general), diminutive of *cerebrum*, brain.]

WHAT THE OTHER WORDS MEAN

cambium: A tissue in the stems and roots of many seed-bearing plants, consisting of cells that divide rapidly to form new layers of tissue.

cerebrum: The large, rounded structure of the brain that fills most of the skull, divided by a deep groove into two parts that are joined at the bottom. It controls thought and voluntary muscular movements.

cesium: A soft, silvery metallic element that is liquid at room temperature and is used in photoelectric cells. The rate of vibration of cesium atoms is used as a standard for measuring time.

tacit

Implied from actions; not spoken or written.

They had a tacit agreement that they would take turns paying for dinner.

[From Latin *tacitus*, silent, past participle of *tacēre*, to be silent.]

WHAT THE OTHER WORDS MEAN

ambiguous: Having two or more possible meanings or interpretations; unclear; vague.

cryptic: Having a hidden meaning or secret nature; mysterious; puzzling.

pallid: Lacking healthy color; pale.

rhizome

A plant stem that grows under or along the ground and that sends out shoots and roots.

Irises can spread rapidly through a garden by their rhizomes.

[From Greek *rhizōma*, mass of roots, from *rhizoun*, to cause to take root, from *rhiza*, root.]

WHAT THE OTHER WORDS MEAN

chloroplast: A tiny structure in the cells of green algae and green plants that contains chlorophyll and creates glucose through photo-synthesis.

phloem: Plant tissue consisting mainly of long, tubular cells through which food is conducted from the leaves to the rest of the plant.

stamen: The male reproductive organ of a flower, usually consisting of a slender stalk with a pollen-bearing part at its tip.

A house standing placidly in the distant fields had to him an ominous look. The shadows of the woods were **formidable**. He was certain that in this vista there lurked fierce-eyed hosts. . . . He glared about him, expecting to see the stealthy approach of his death.

—Stephen Crane
The Red Badge of Courage

formidable

Arousing fear, dread, or alarm.

He wanted to audition for the play, but the formidable prospect of appearing in front of a large audience made him hesitate.

[From Middle English *formydable*, from Old French *formidable*, from Latin *formīdābilis*, from *formīdāre*, to fear, from *formīdō*, fear.]

WHAT THE OTHER WORDS MEAN

dubious: Arousing doubt; doubtful.

incendiary: Arousing anger or conflict; inflammatory.

noisome: Offensive to the point of arousing disgust; foul.

54.

asymptote

A line whose distance to a given curve gets closer and closer to zero.

In geometry class we learned that an asymptote may or may not intersect its associated curve.

[Ultimately from Greek *asumptōtos*, not intersecting : *a-*, not + *sumptōtos*, intersecting (from *sumpiptein*, *sumptō-*, to converge : *sun-*, syn- + *piptein*, to fall).]

WHAT THE OTHER WORDS MEAN

axis: A straight line about which a body or geometric object rotates or may be conceived to rotate.

focus: A point at which rays of light come together or from which they appear to spread apart, as after passing through a lens.

theorem: A mathematical statement whose truth can be proved on the basis of a given set of axioms or assumptions.

dendrite

A branching part of a nerve cell that receives and transmits cell impulses.

Most neurons have more than one dendrite.

[From Greek *dendrītēs*, of or relating to a tree, from *dendron*, tree.]

WHAT THE OTHER WORDS MEAN

axon: The long extension of a nerve cell that carries impulses away from the body of the cell.

boron: A brown or black nonmetallic element extracted chiefly from borax and occurring as a powder or hard crystalline solid. It is used in hard alloys, nuclear reactors, and abrasives.

ganglion: A compact group of nerve cells forming a nerve center, especially one located outside the brain or spinal cord.

moratorium

A stopping of some activity for the time being; a temporary ban or pause.

The activists called for a moratorium on buying clothes manufactured in sweatshops until the workers' conditions were improved.

[From Late Latin *morātōrium*, neuter of Latin *morātōrius*, causing delay, from *morātōrī*, *morāt-*, to delay, from *mora*, a pause, delay.]

WHAT THE OTHER WORDS MEAN

crematorium: A furnace or building with a furnace for burning corpses.

natatorium: An indoor swimming pool.

sanatorium: An institution for the treatment of chronic diseases.

57.

epaulet

A shoulder ornament, especially a fringed strap worn on military uniforms.

The officer appeared at the ceremony in full dress uniform, complete with an epaulet on her shoulder and sword by her side.

[From French *épaulette*, diminutive of *épaule*, shoulder, from Old French *espaule*, from Late Latin *spatula*, shoulder blade.]

WHAT THE OTHER WORDS MEAN

epitaph: An inscription on a tombstone or monument in memory of the person buried there.

epoch: A period, especially one in history marked by certain important events or developments; an era.

epsilon: The fifth letter of the Greek alphabet.

58.

sanguine

Cheerfully confident; optimistic.

Despite several rejections, the author was sanguine about eventually finding a publisher.

[From Middle English, from Old French *sanguin,* blood-red, ruddy, sanguine, from Latin *sanguineus,* bloody, from *sanguis, sanguin-,* blood.]

WHAT THE OTHER WORDS MEAN

choleric: Easily made angry; bad-tempered.

melancholy: Sad; gloomy.

phlegmatic: Having or suggesting a calm, sluggish temperament; unemotional.

Observing the similarity in form between **sanguine**, "cheerfully optimistic," and *sanguinary*, "bloodthirsty," we may wonder why the words have such different meanings. The explanation lies in the medieval theory of the four humors, or bodily fluids, called blood, bile, phlegm, and black bile. A person's temperament was determined by the relative proportions of the humors in the body. When blood was the predominant humor, a person had a ruddy face and a disposition marked by courage, hope, and a readiness to fall in love. In Middle English, the word used to describe such a person was *sanguine* (the ancestor of the Modern English word). Middle English *sanguine* came from Old French *sanguin*, "blood-colored, ruddy, having a sanguine temperament," and Old French *sanguin* in turn descended from the Latin adjective *sanguineus*, "bloody, blood-colored." Latin *sanguineus* itself was derived from the Latin noun *sanguis*, "blood." *Sanguis* was also the source of another adjective, *sanguinārius*, "having to do with blood," that is the ultimate source of English *sanguinary*.

Define-a-Thon
Answer Key

1. veranda
2. meticulous
3. infallible
4. fulminate
5. basilisk
6. intermittent
7. undulate
8. diurnal
9. liniment
10. stirrup
11. typhoon
12. cosine
13. endorphin
14. sobriquet
15. palindrome
16. obfuscate
17. duodecimal
18. promontory
19. stultify
20. treason
21. aseptic
22. effervescence
23. reprove
24. barcarole
25. protoplasm
26. codicil
27. affidavit
28. ginkgo
29. carillon
30. exegesis
31. quash
32. palanquin
33. fusty
34. intermezzo
35. inertia
36. fibrillate
37. vitality
38. malcontent
39. googol
40. firewall
41. cartel
42. femur
43. iconoclast
44. quiescent
45. astrolabe
46. ichthyology
47. motif
48. countenance
49. cadence
50. cerebellum
51. tacit
52. rhizome
53. formidable
54. asymptote
55. dendrite
56. moratorium
57. epaulet
58. sanguine